CANADA'S WETLAND ANIMALS

Chelsea Donaldson

Scholastic Canada Ltd.

Toronto New York London Auckland Sydney
Mexico City New Delhi Hong Kong Buenos Aires

Scholastic Canada Ltd.
175 Hillmount Road, Markham, Ontario L6C 1Z7, Canada
Scholastic Inc.
557 Broadway, New York, NY 10012, USA
Scholastic Australia Pty Limited
PO Box 579, Gosford, NSW 2250, Australia
Scholastic New Zealand Limited
Private Bag 94407, Greenmount, Auckland, New Zealand
Scholastic Ltd.
Villiers House, Clarendon Avenue, Leamington Spa,
Warwickshire CV32 5PR, UK

Every reasonable effort has been made to trace the ownership of copyright material used in the text. The publisher would be pleased to know of any errors or omissions.

Visual Credits
Cover, pp. i (border), iii (border): W. Lynch/Ivy Images; pp. i, 12, 14, 16–17, 26: Thomas Kitchin & Victoria Hurst; p. iv (map): Hothouse Canada; pp. iv–1: Courtesy of the National Oceanic and Atmospheric Administration Central Library Photo Collection; pp. 2–3: Leonard Lee Rue/maxx-images.com; pp. 4, 27, 29, 30, 31, 33, 34, 38, 40: © Dwight Kuhn; p. 5: Hemera/maxximages.com; p. 6: Peter Weimann/maxximages.com; pp. 8, 13, 15, 24, 37, 39, 41, 43: Bill Ivy; p. 9: Alan & Sandy Carey/Ivy Images; p. 11: Superstock/maxximages.com; p. 18: Mark Hunt/maxximages.com; pp. 19, 21: W. Lankinen/Ivy Images; p. 20: Rich Reid/maxximages.com; p. 22: Dick Hemingway Editorial Photographs; p. 23: © 1988 S. Nielsen/DRK Photo; p. 25: © 1996 S. Nielsen/DRK Photo; p. 36: © Lang Elliott/NatureSound Studio, www.naturesound.com; p. 42: Oliver Meckes/Nicole Ottawa/Photo Researchers, Inc/Firstlight.ca; p. 44 (all): U.S. Fish & Wildlife Service

Produced by Focus Strategic Communications Inc.
Project Management and Editorial: Adrianna Edwards
Design and Layout: Lisa Platt
Photo Research: Elizabeth Kelly

Special thanks to Dr. Bill Freedman of Dalhousie University for his expertise.

Library and Archives Canada Cataloguing in Publication
Donaldson, Chelsea, 1959-
Canada's wetland animals / Chelsea Donaldson.
(Canada close up)
ISBN 0-439-95675-7
1. Wetland animals—Canada—Juvenile literature.
I. Title. II. Series: Canada close up (Markham, Ont.)
QL113.8.65 2006   j591.768'0971   C2005-904140-4

6 5 4 3 2 1   Printed in Canada   06 07 08 09

TABLE OF CONTENTS

Canada's Wetlands

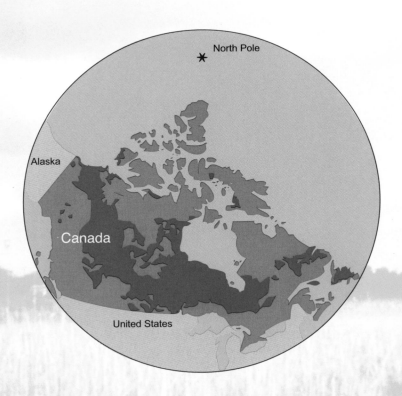

North Pole

Alaska

Canada

United States

■ Densest/Largest Canadian Wetlands

■ Canada

□ United States

Welcome to the Wetlands!

Canada has 25% of the world's wetlands. They can be found all over the country. Some are large, and others are small. But all wetlands are very important to the environment.

Wetlands are areas that are part land and part water. They are often very muddy and may be covered in water for all or part of the year. Swamps, marshes, bogs and fens are all types of wetlands that can be found in Canada.

Canada's wetlands are not good places for people to live. They are often soggy, mucky and full of bugs. But wetlands are still packed with life! Lots of plants and animals do live there. Let's meet some of these creatures.

CHAPTER ONE

Beaver

Beavers don't just *live* in wetlands.
Sometimes they help create them!
They do this by damming streams.

A beaver dam is like a wall made of
branches, mud and grass. When the dam
is big enough, the water can't get through.
It creates a deep pond where the beaver
can build its home.

After a while, wetland plants
start to grow around the pond.
Then other wetland
creatures come there
to live. A new wetland
area is born.

Beavers are great builders. Besides dams, they also build their homes. These are called beaver lodges. Beavers use their sharp front teeth to cut down trees. Then they drag the twigs and branches to the edge of the water. They build walls and plaster them with grass and mud to make them strong. Then they cover their homes with dome-shaped roofs.

From the outside, the lodge looks like a rounded pile of sticks. All the entrances are hidden under water. But inside is a dry, comfortable room big enough for a whole beaver family.

A male and a female beaver usually stay together their whole lives. Every spring three or four babies, called kits, are born in the lodge. The young beavers stay with their parents for up to two years. As they grow, the beavers help to look after their younger brothers and sisters. They are one big happy family!

A beaver's body is well suited to life in the wetlands. A beaver has webbed hind feet and a wide, flat tail to help it swim. Special flaps keep water out of its ears, nose and mouth. A beaver can swim underwater for up to 15 minutes at a time! Its thick fur coat keeps the cold away, even in icy winter weather.

The tail has other uses as well. The beaver uses it for balance while gnawing or dragging trees. And when the beaver senses danger, it slaps its tail on the water to warn its relatives to stay away.

CHAPTER TWO

River Otter

Have you ever gone down a waterslide? It can be a lot of fun.

River otters like slides too. They often make their own in the banks of rivers. They spend hours sliding down into the water. Otters love to play.

The other thing otters love to do is eat. Luckily, they are great hunters. Otters usually dine on fish, but they also hunt insects, frogs and small animals, such as muskrats.

Sometimes they even catch birds. When a bird lands on the water, an otter can sneak up from below and grab it.

An otter is completely at home in the water. A layer of air trapped in its fur helps keep it afloat, just like a life jacket.

An otter can even sleep and eat while floating on its back. No other land mammal can float, swim and dive as well as an otter.

Otters often make their homes in abandoned beaver lodges, old muskrat dens or hollow logs near riverbanks. In the spring, one, two, three or even four babies, called cubs, are born in the den.

The cubs have big heads, thin tails and lots of fur to keep them warm. They are blind for about a month after they are born. But almost as soon as their eyes open, they are ready to swim, play and explore.

CHAPTER THREE

Moose

Moose depend on wetlands for survival. In summer, they spend most of their time standing in the water, eating and keeping cool. They love to eat the plants and trees that grow in and around the water.

Water also keeps a moose safe from wolves and bears. A moose can stand in deep water on its long legs. But its enemies have to swim.

Moose are giants. They are the largest land animals in Canada. A male moose, or bull, can weigh as much as six full-grown men. And those antlers make it look even bigger!

A bull moose's antlers drop off in the winter and grow back every spring. Sometimes one side will fall off before the other. Then the moose has to walk around with its head pulled over to one side!

Most of the time, moose live quiet lives
alone. But all that changes for a few
weeks in the fall. That is when moose look
for mates. Mating time is known as the
rut. During the rut, bull moose sometimes
attack people, cars and even trains!

To attract a mate, a bull moose claims a
part of the forest as his territory and
chases away smaller bulls. If an invading
bull does not leave, the animals may fight
with their antlers. Sometimes the antlers
get tangled. Unless they can pull them
apart, both bulls will die.

Calves stay with their mothers for about a year. But about half of all moose calves die before they are one year old. Most are killed by bears or wolves. Others starve during the long winter.

Never get between a moose cow and her calf. The mother won't stop to ask if you are friendly. She will just charge. Since an adult moose can run very fast, it's a good idea to stay clear!

CHAPTER FOUR

Great Blue Heron

Birds love Canada's wetlands. The plants that grow there give them a safe place to build nests. The many insects, animals and fish that live there provide them with plenty of food.

Herons are big fans of wetlands. There are lots of different kinds of herons. But the biggest of all is the great blue heron. This bird stands about a metre tall. It has a long bill and even longer legs. It looks like it is walking on stilts. The feathers on its back, wings and abdomen are a greyish-blue colour. There is a dark blue patch on its shoulders.

How long can you stand on one leg?
A great blue heron can balance like that
for hours. It can even sleep in this
position. It locks one knee and tucks the
other leg underneath its belly.

A heron's knees bend backwards instead
of forwards, as ours do. When a heron
kneels down, its feet are in front of it,
not behind!

A heron is a
great fisher.
It stands very still
by the edge of the
water and waits for fish
to swim by. Then it snatches
a fish in its bill. It flips the
catch around so it is holding
it longways, and lets
the fish slide headfirst
down its throat
— in one piece!

Sometimes herons stand near people
who are fishing to beg for a free meal.
But most of the time, herons prefer to
hunt by themselves.

Herons are more social when they are nesting. In fact, tens or even hundreds of herons may nest together in a colony. Both parents help to make the nest in a tree. They also take turns sitting on the eggs and finding food for the babies when they hatch.

If you ever come across a heron colony, stay well back. Herons often leave their eggs if people come too close. Then the babies will die.

CHAPTER FIVE

Common Loon

If you are ever near a lake on a summers night, stop and listen. You may hear a kind of crazy laughing sound. Or maybe a soft, sad wail. Both of these strange calls are made by the common loon.

You will probably hear the loon before you see it. This bird is careful to stay out of sight. It sometimes hides from people and other predators by sinking down low in the water. Only its head and bill stick out.

But it is very easy to spot loons when they are taking off or landing on the water. Loons need to pick up speed before they take off. To do this, they run across the surface of the water, with their wings flapping, until they are moving fast enough to fly.

When landing, loons touch down on the water at very high speeds. They spray water with their feet, just like a water skier.

After choosing a mate, loons often stay together for life. Both the male and the female build the nest and take turns sitting on the eggs until they hatch.

After the babies are born, both parents help to feed them. Although the chicks can swim right away, they often hitch a ride on Mom or Dad's back!

CHAPTER SIX

Mallard Duck

Have you ever seen ducks swimming in a pond at a park? The ducks in the park are tame. They are used to living around people.

But other ducks live in the wild, away from people. Many are found in Canada's wetlands. They like to live in lakes, rivers, ponds or marshes.

The mallard duck is one of the most common types of duck in Canada.

It is easy to tell a male mallard from a female. The male has a beautiful yellow bill, a green head and a white ring around its neck that looks just like a necktie. These bright colours help it to attract a female.

The female is much less showy. She has plain brown feathers that blend in with the grasses and reeds around the water's edge. She does not want to attract any attention while she is sitting on the nest.

If you watch a mallard long enough, you will see its head suddenly disappear under the water. Its tail will stick straight up in the air. It looks as if it is doing a headstand in the water!

This is called dabbling. Mallards dip under the surface to grab underwater plants. They have special bills that allow them to hold on to their food while water drains out the sides of their bills.

Because mallards have no teeth, they can't chew. Instead, they swallow grit and sand after they eat to help them grind up their food.

Mallard nests need to be well hidden. Duck eggs make a tasty meal for raccoons, crows, skunks and weasels. Wetland grasses and reeds provide a perfect hiding place.

Almost as soon as the chicks hatch, their mother leads them to the water. One by one, they plop into the water. They can start swimming right away!

CHAPTER SEVEN

Snapping Turtle

What animal has no teeth but still has a wicked bite? It's the same animal that lives in the water but hardly swims — the snapping turtle!

Snapping turtles are the largest freshwater turtles in Canada. Their shells grow about as big as the head of a tennis racquet.

They are also one of the oldest creatures on the planet. Their ancestors first walked the Earth about 75 million years before the dinosaurs!

Snapping turtles spend most of their lives in shallow water. They are so heavy that it is hard for them to swim. Instead, they walk along the bottom of the lake, pond or stream.

In winter, snappers sink beneath the water's surface and dig themselves into the mud to hibernate. While they are sleeping, they do not breathe for up to six months!

Like most turtles, a snapper has two shells. The hard shell on the top is called a *carapace* (CARE-i-pace). The softer shell underneath is called a *plastron* (PLAS-tren).

Most turtles pull inside their shells for protection. Snappers can't do that because their plastrons are too small to fit their feet, legs and heads. On the other hand, they can run much more quickly because their legs have more room to move.

So how does a snapper defend itself? By snapping, of course! Although it has no teeth, a snapping turtle has a razor-sharp beak that can lock onto a finger. Once locked on, it can be very hard to get the turtle to open up. The snapper can even bite a finger off!

In the summer, snapping turtles leave the water to mate. The mother digs a hole and lays up to 30 eggs. She covers the hole with earth and then goes back to the water, never to return to that nest.

Sometimes the eggs are eaten by other animals, such as foxes or skunks. If the eggs do hatch, the young turtles are only about as big as a quarter. They run for the water as fast as their little legs will take them. Even so, most of them don't make it. They are grabbed by hungry birds or other animals. It's not easy being a baby snapping turtle!

CHAPTER EIGHT

Crayfish

Crayfish are funny-looking creatures. They have two short and two long antennae. Their small, beady eyes sit on the ends of short stalks that can move in all directions. They have two claws, eight legs, a fan-shaped tail and a hard outer shell.

Crayfish live in the shallow water of lakes, ponds, rivers, streams and swamps. Some even live in fields that are flooded with water.

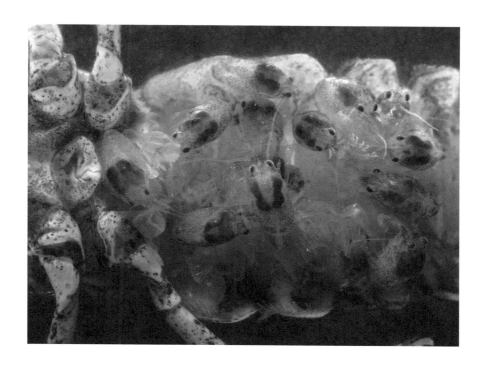

Crayfish are born from eggs that look like little black berries. The mother glues the eggs to the bottom of the back section of her body. A mother crayfish who is carrying her eggs is said to be "in berry."

When the eggs hatch, the babies stay attached for a while until they are big enough to look after themselves.

How much have you grown in the past year? You are probably growing all the time. Luckily, your skin stretches to fit. And all you have to do is wear larger clothes.

For a young crayfish, it's a little different. It grows out of its skin. As a crayfish grows, its shell stays the same size. Every few weeks, it has to shed its old shell and wait for the new one to harden. This is called moulting. Even when a crayfish is grown, it has to moult every so often.

Crayfish eat almost anything — plants, small fish, worms and even other crayfish. Some species help to keep lakes and rivers clean by eating the remains of dead animals.

To escape its predators, a crayfish may
run away or wave its claws around. Or it
may swim backwards by flipping its back
end like a big fin. If that doesn't work,
it has another trick. If an animal grabs
one of the crayfish's legs, the crayfish just
breaks the leg off and scuttles away. Soon
enough, the missing leg will grow back!

CHAPTER NINE

Bullfrog

One of the predators that crayfish try to avoid is the bullfrog. A bullfrog may not look very fierce to us. But to many small wetland animals, the bullfrog is a very scary neighbour! A bullfrog eats whatever it can fit in its mouth. It can gulp down an insect, another frog or even a newly hatched duckling.

Bullfrogs are the largest frogs in Canada. They can grow up to 20 centimetres long. And they can leap almost 10 times that far. Imagine if you could jump 10 times your own length!

Bullfrogs like wetland areas mostly because of the plants that grow in the water. These plants create areas with slow-moving water. Female bullfrogs like to lay their eggs there.

Bullfrogs mate in the spring and early summer. If you visit a pond or wetland then, you can hear the male frogs singing together in chorus. They make a deep croaking sound. It sounds like the noise you hear when you blow into a large jug.

They are calling out to female bullfrogs and warning other males to stay away from their territory.

Female frogs lay about 20,000 eggs!
Their eggs float near the top of the water.
In about four days, the baby bullfrogs
hatch. They are called tadpoles.

The tiny tadpoles don't look anything like
an adult bullfrog. They have big heads
and long tails but no legs. It will take
them about three years to grow into their
adult shape. Until then, they will have to
avoid all kinds of predators, including
other bullfrogs. Only a few of the tadpoles
will live to become adults.

CHAPTER TEN

Dragonfly

Dragonflies are among the best flyers in the insect world. Just like many birds, dragonflies can stop, start, hover and move backward or forward very quickly. They even eat while they are in the air. Since their favourite food is mosquitoes, dragonflies are very useful to have around!

Dragonflies in the air are very beautiful. In the sunlight, their long bodies and lacy wings seem to have tiny rainbows of colours. But did you know that these amazing flyers spend most of their lives as plain, brown, wingless underwater insects?

Dragonflies hatch in the water and may stay there for up to three years. This part of the dragonfly life cycle is called the *nymph* (NIMF) stage.

A dragonfly nymph has gills like a fish to help it breathe underwater. It has a hard outer shell that it moults as it grows, just like crayfish do.

As the nymph gets older, its eyes get bigger. It starts to develop the beginnings of wings.

Then one night,
the nymph crawls up
the stem of a plant.
It leaves its watery
world and enters the
world of air and light.
Soon its shell cracks
open and the new
creature inside wriggles
its way out. Around
dawn, the dragonfly is
ready to try out its
amazing wings for
the first time.

Sadly, by now most of the dragonfly's life is over. It will only live in the air for about six weeks. During that time, it mates with another dragonfly. The eggs are laid in the water, and the cycle begins again.

CHAPTER ELEVEN

Leech

Do you like earthworms? Do you ever watch them crawling in the dirt? Earthworms have cousins. They're called leeches.

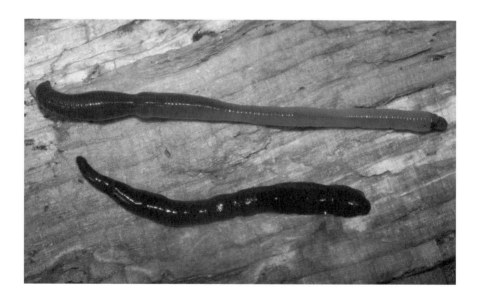

In some ways, leeches are very much like earthworms. They have long, soft bodies and no legs. But leeches are different from earthworms in some important ways.

For one thing, many leeches live in water, not underground. And unlike earthworms, leeches have suction cups around their mouths and tails.

Some leeches use their suckers to attach themselves to fish or other animals. They make a hole in their prey's skin and suck its blood. Leeches may sound like scary vampires, but the animals often don't even notice the leeches attached to them.

As leeches feed, they get bigger ... and bigger ... and bigger! When they are finally full, they just drop off and swim away.

Sometimes leeches will even attach themselves to human skin. If you ever find a leech on your skin after swimming, don't panic! Just sprinkle some salt on it, and it will drop off.

Did you know that leeches can be very useful? If someone loses a finger or toe, doctors may be able to reattach it. But sometimes too much blood rushes to the wound. Leeches can take away some of the extra blood and help the wound to heal!

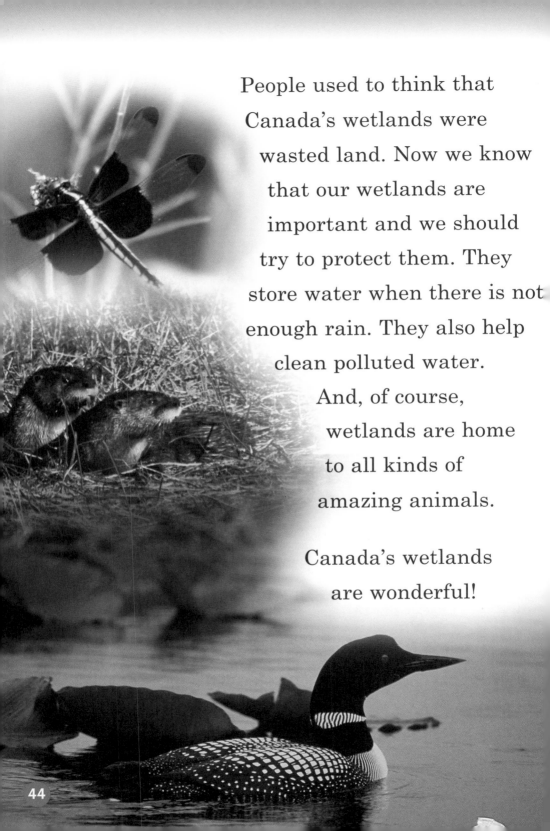

People used to think that Canada's wetlands were wasted land. Now we know that our wetlands are important and we should try to protect them. They store water when there is not enough rain. They also help clean polluted water.

And, of course, wetlands are home to all kinds of amazing animals.

Canada's wetlands are wonderful!